Aphids

by Colleen Sexton

BLASTOFF! READERS
2

BELLWETHER MEDIA • MINNEAPOLIS, MN

Note to Librarians, Teachers, and Parents:

Blastoff! Readers are carefully developed by literacy experts and combine standards-based content with developmentally appropriate text.

Level 1 provides the most support through repetition of high-frequency words, light text, predictable sentence patterns, and strong visual support.

Level 2 offers early readers a bit more challenge through varied simple sentences, increased text load, and less repetition of high-frequency words.

Level 3 advances early-fluent readers toward fluency through increased text and concept load, less reliance on visuals, longer sentences, and more literary language.

Level 4 builds reading stamina by providing more text per page, increased use of punctuation, greater variation in sentence patterns, and increasingly challenging vocabulary.

Level 5 encourages children to move from "learning to read" to "reading to learn" by providing even more text, varied writing styles, and less familiar topics.

Whichever book is right for your reader, Blastoff! Readers are the perfect books to build confidence and encourage a love of reading that will last a lifetime!

This edition first published in 2009 by Bellwether Media.

No part of this publication may be reproduced in whole or in part without written permission of the publisher. For information regarding permission, write to Bellwether Media Inc., Attention: Permissions Department, Post Office Box 19349, Minneapolis, MN 55419.

Library of Congress Cataloging-in-Publication Data
Sexton, Colleen A., 1967–
    Aphids / by Colleen Sexton.
        p. cm. – (Blastoff! readers. World of insects)
    Includes bibliographical references and index.
    Summary: "Simple text and full color photographs introduce beginning readers to aphids. Developed by literacy experts for students in kindergarten through third grade"–Provided by publisher.
    ISBN-13: 978-1-60014-189-8 (hardcover : alk. paper)
    ISBN-10: 1-60014-189-7 (hardcover : alk. paper)
    1. Aphids–Juvenile literature. I. Title.

    QL527.A64S46 2008
    595.7'52–dc22   2008019870

Contents

Aphids are tiny **insects**.

One aphid could fit on the
head of a pin.

Aphids live on the leaves of trees and other plants.

Thousands of aphids can live on one plant.

Most aphids are green or black. They can also be red, yellow, or other colors.

Some aphids have a fuzzy wax covering that looks like cotton. It helps keep aphids warm and dry.

9

Aphids have a soft body
and a small head.

Some aphids have wings.
They can fly from plant to plant.

Aphids have six thin, weak legs. They do not walk far.

antennas

Aphids have two **antennas**. They use their antennas to feel and smell.

mouth

An aphid's mouth is shaped like a tube. Aphids suck plant juices through their mouths.

Aphids can make plants sick.
Some plants stop growing
and their leaves curl.

15

tubes

Aphids have two tubes on their body. A juice called **honeydew** flows out of these tubes.

Honeydew drips and forms a
sticky coating where it lands.

Ants eat the sweet honeydew.
Aphids let ants collect
honeydew from their bodies.

Ants take care of aphids in return. Ants carry aphids to new plants that they can eat.

Ants protect aphids from ladybugs and other **predators**.

Aphids and ants need
each other!

Glossary

antennas—the feelers on an insect's head; insects use their antennas to touch and smell things.

honeydew—a sweet, sticky liquid made by aphids and some other insects

insect—a small animal with six legs and a body divided into three parts; there are more insects in the world than any other kind of animal.

predator—an animal that hunts other animals for food

To Learn More

AT THE LIBRARY

Goppel, Christine. *Anna Aphid*. New York: North-South Books, 2005.

Mound, Laurence. *Insect*. New York: DK Publishing, 2007.

O'Neill, Amanda. *Insects and Bugs*. New York: Kingfisher, 2002.

ON THE WEB

Learning more about aphids is as easy as 1, 2, 3.

1. Go to www.factsurfer.com

2. Enter "aphids" into search box.

3. Click the "Surf" button and you will see a list of related web sites.

With factsurfer.com, finding more information is just a click away.

Index

The images in this book are reproduced through the courtesy of: Witold Ryka, front cover, p. 11; Laura Stone, p. 4; Michael Pettigrew, p. 5; Emilio Ereza / age fotostock, p. 6; Phil Degginger / Alamy, p 7; Bartomeu Borrell / age fotostock, p. 8; blickwinkel / Almay, p. 9; Nigel Cattlin / Alamy, pp. 10, 15; pixelman, p. 12; O.DIGOIT / Alamy, pp. 13, 16-17; Geoff du Feu / age fotostock, p. 14; Danita Delimont / Alamy, pp. 18-19; Antje Schulte / Alamy, p. 20; Arco Images GmbH / Alamy, p. 21.